THE EDUCATIONAL PLEDGE:
Questions to Self-Development
By Alberto O. Cappas

Edited by
Solomon Joseph

ISBN: 9781793894908

Published in cooperation with The Educational Pledge
Latinovillage1@gmail.com
theeducationalpledge@gmail.com

buffalolatinovillage.com
theeducationalpledge.com

*"Children must be
taught how to think, not what to think."*

Margaret Mead

You don't need permission to think!

TURN ON THE LIGHT

The material works best when mentors, parents, counselors, and teachers interact with students in using this handbook.

A lesson plan or classroom discussion will go a long way in actualizing the connection to the mental light.

A book to share with youth at risk who are mentally trapped inside the box.

Dedicated to the wings of my mother

Content

Introduction
By Solomon Joseph

It is often said that to be great you must overcome many obstacles, that only the strong survive, and that only those who possess the power of the mind, can create success for themselves.

Nothing can be further from the truth when you're honest with yourself, and when you learn to empower yourself by answering your own questions about life.

"The Educational Pledge" is a guide for survival, a book I've read and adopted as a guide for myself. It has taught me how education can be used as a tool to further your goals in life.

The author, Alberto O. Cappas, has helped me to realize the importance of education and why we need to empower ourselves. The "Educational Pledge", which is included in this book, is a self-development pledge designed to help us understand how we can begin to empower ourselves.

I've been confused growing up because I didn't know which way I was going, and which way I wanted to go. When I read the "Pledge", I finally found meaning in the type of person I wanted to be. After all these years, I was finally convinced that it's never too late to make a U-turn. My mission in life is to help educate each other about the world, and how connected we really are.

I was fortunate to come across Alberto Cappas, when I picked up a copy of the Latino Village, a publication he co-publishes with his wife, Ramona.

I followed up by contacting him, to meet the person responsible for the "Educational Pledge." He immediately introduced me to his life's work. and I completely connected with him.

I've always believed that we are constantly learning and that we can always learn more, especially if we just relax and open our heart. I began to read the Educational Pledge, daily and began answering very deep questions about myself, my goals and how I can establish an example in life.

I believe everyone should take the time to reflect on who they are, and what they can become. I have applied the Educational Pledge to my life, and sharing it with others, helps me to empower them, and it gives me great joy.

It gives me hope that we can help many others - men, women, and children of all ages, to understand the meaning of their lives. We live in an age where it's easy to lose track of who we are, and where we're going and makes many of us feel like it's too late to get back on track -- but it's not!

What you hold in your hands is a guide to help you understand who you are and how you can empower yourself. Please take the time to be grateful for the life you have and for the life you are about to live.

Take the Pledge, Empower yourself!

Why the Book

The book is based on my many years of speaking to young people and others about the need to take control of our lives and not allow politicians, rap musicians, teachers, family members, and negative forces to make decisions or choices for our paths in life; they are prominent images and realities we face every day in our communities, as well as in the media and fashion industry.

The work is based on educating young people to understand the meaning and definition of **values and standards** in one's life. The more we understand its meaning, the more control we will have over the choices we make in life. When one instills these values and standards as a system within oneself, one has a better change at leading a more productive and meaningful journey in his or her lifetime.

For example, society instills in our young people that they must go to school to prepare for a job that would lead to a career. I strongly believe and know from personal experience that we must go much further in convincing our young people why education is so important.

Education is a very important tool. However, to share that importance, one cannot display or emphasize one reason, which has become a negative reaction to many of our young people. Our young people must be made aware of other dynamics for pursuing an education.

We must instill in our young people that they must go to school for other important reasons, such as: learning to read, learning to write, an opportunity to meet other human beings outside their immediate social or neighborhood circle, exposure to the arts, providing him or her a stage to be exposed to other cultures and customs.

We need to pay attention to a young person's positive hobbies, to see how we can help him or her make an intellectual connection between their skills and the amazing business and economic potential of their hobbies. This hobby can prepare them to become providers rather than consumers.

If we can provide this awareness, this motivation, the love for education will increase, and the school dropout rate will decrease.

I dropped out of school several times until someone took the time and introduced me to the world of art, theatre, and poetry, giving me a reason to go back to school and pursue my education. I no longer felt as if I was being forced to go to school only to prepare for a job. I became aware that school was a beginning to my personal growth and development, and not to a job, I started to understand and appreciate the true meaning of the word, "education."

The Educational Pledge provides young people with the chance and opportunity to visualize these inner qualities at an early stage, to understand that although they do not see it, a conceptual system (ideas, values, and standards) does exist for them to visualize – even within the midst of a negative environment (poor schools, gangs, inner cities, et). This book is not only limited to young people. It applies to older people or students as well. It is never too late to make a U-turn.

It is vital that role models, mentors, teachers, parents, and youth-serving professionals help young people understand this book and help them to examine their purpose on the planet and to begin to discuss and define the meaning of ideas, values, and standards essential to one's personal growth and development. There should be no judgments attached. This should be an open conversation where the young person knows that there are no "wrong or right" answers. It is a time to openly bring out the individual's honest comments without judgment from the onset. The facilitator should open the discussion with a "non-judgment" policy as the ground rule.

I first wrote the poem, **The Educational Pledge,** which I used in my poetry readings to young audiences in public schools, colleges, community organizations, and corrections. It is designed to serve as a guide to help one understand and navigate the daily encounters and activities in our lives. The poem, as a stand-alone piece, has been widely published and used in newspapers, magazines, flyers, book form, bookmarks, videos, internet, and by individuals and organizations.

The direct audience for this book is the young people in urban communities, students and their parents, school counselors, teachers, and educational consultants.

Individual students can utilize this book as an "everyday guide." It can be used as a one-on-one counseling tool by the teacher, counselor, or parents, and it is an excellent source for group discussions, workshops, and seminars. It would make a great curriculum for a school.

CONNECTING WITH THE UNIVERSE

I plan to have an opportunity to help you light up the areas you need to light up, as well as to turn off the areas you need to turn off. It is my belief that to succeed in life, to enjoy the time we spend on this planet, to be in control of where we need to be or where we plan to be or where we would like to be, we first need to have a plan of balance in our lives.

Balance is a part of the purpose for our journey. I have been able to lead a decent and honorable life, completing several episodes that in the scheme of this life, do not seem to go together, especially when it comes to functioning as a poet/writer, community activist, entrepreneur, government official, art gallery owner, and publisher.

Early in my career, when I lived in Buffalo, NY before moving back to New York City, I served as a deputy commissioner for the New York State Division for Youth (Communications & Special Projects).

In New York City, I worked as director of community affairs for the Health & Hospitals Corporation, and from there I moved to the NYC Human Resources Administration (HRA) as their deputy commission (Community Affairs & City-wide Community Boards).

Prior to these positions, I served as associate director of Minority Affairs for the State University of NY at Buffalo, a position I accepted upon my graduation from the same institution.

All these institutions are massive organizations. The key for my growth and development as a human being is that I stayed focus on my love to serve people. In all the above positions, they all related to public service – a love I've never compromised.

I was born in Puerto Rico, raised in New York City, in a single parent household. My home life consisted of five sisters and two other brothers, all raised under the influence and negative images of welfare, food stamps, government cheese, peanut butter, and buster brown shoes. At an early age, I found myself on the receiving end as a consumer of government's public assistance programs.

My outside environment included gangs on every corner recruiting new victims to display their "macho egos." I experienced people drinking themselves to death, lovers betraying each other, and young people destroying their lives with drugs. I witnessed Puerto Ricans, Blacks, and poor Whites coming together to form gangs to fight other Puerto Ricans, Blacks, and poor Whites.

I witnessed many of my peers dropping out of school, denouncing education and refusing to learn and advance themselves.

Education was not cool – so my neighborhood friends elected to stay in the Box, an invisible and negative consuming space that produced manipulation of their lives without their input. It was an early age beginning, decisions and choices traveling in the wrong direction, stopping on ignorance and personal apathy Avenues.

Today the Box continues to be an invisible but powerful force, a system of mental traffic signs directing and pushing our young people in different directions without their awareness or approval.

A state of mind...

Once within the Box, the captive is without a concrete philosophical or spiritual purpose, no foundation to stand tall in the face of society. This is a dangerous imbalance.

I was fortunate that at an early age, I could see things clearly. It took me awhile to understand and properly use this clear vision. I knew that something was not right, something was terribly wrong in the way we were just living our lives from day-to-day, without thinking of the impact of our decision and choices. We never considered the consequences of our choices and decisions. I was inside the Box.

I noticed that most the Italians and Irish families had jobs. My family was on welfare. My Black and Puerto Rican friends were also on welfare. We accepted the government cheese, the ham, the dry milk, and the peanut butter, as well as Buster Brown shoes. We never questioned why.

We were a complete mess and we did not know it.

The Box.

Even today many of us are still inside the Box, and still on the road to nowhere. This is a dangerous imbalance. As a Puerto Rican coming to a new land, a new language, and a cold climate, I became certain of my presence in the USA mainland, uncertain of my worth as a human being, and in the process of dealing with USA mainland institutions, I lost the identity of who I was as a Puerto Rican. Consequently, I also lost my self-esteem and eventually started disliking myself. This is a dangerous imbalance.

Fortunately, the self-hatred did not last long…

Due to not going to school, I was labeled a PIN (Person in Need of Supervision) at the age of fourteen. The Juvenile Justice System confined me to reform school for troubled youth. I was sent to a place called the Warwick State Training School for Boys, in upstate, NY where everything was green, removing me from the destructive inner-city elements --- a geographic change.

The experience of going from New York City streets to a new environmental setting in upstate, NY, opened a door to a whole new world. At that moment, I realized that the world was composed of more than just one part, and not just the streets that were consuming me.

When I was in public school, I used to read about "Dick and Jane", thinking they were a figment of someone's imagination because their lives and neighborhood was nothing like mine. But I found out that they were real, along with the beautiful farm, barns, cows, pigs, and horses. This was the beginning of developing my inner structure for Balance.

I also learned or discovered that I was a smart and creative individual. While in confinement, many of the White, Black, and Latino youth paid me in cigarettes and other items for me to write letters to their girlfriends and families when they discovered I had my way with words, and with a pen. This was an educational and intellectual awakening for me, to have all these people come to me, to depend on me, to write or read for them due to their inability to read or write. This experience alone broke the "colonial mentality" inside of me. The lack of self-esteem and self-hatred literally disappeared completely. This was for me a regaining of Balance.

As great as this country might be (many believe that it is regardless of its cruel history), many of us have lost sight of the true values of one's life journey, placing too much emphasis on financial wants over one's need for good health, good friends, social enjoyment, spending quality time with our family members, and truly enjoying the work or career we find ourselves. Balance.

We should truly listen to the saying: "You can't pay me enough to be miserable." Think about this quote very carefully. If we have not learned or know the meaning of this quote, start today, become wise and begin to learn the essence of the words before our journey ends. It is never too late to make a U-turn to regain our Balance.

I know too many people who now regret holding on to their twenty-year plus jobs to be eligible for retirement and a pension. In waiting for the pension plan, they grew old and tired letting dreams pass them bye, allowing them to disappear. If they had to do it again, they would take the risk, and not the stability of a 9-5. Balance.

At times, we also make decisions or choices for the wrong reasons. For example, I want more money, so I will take a job that would pay me more, knowing full well that I will be miserable in the job, leading to stress and perhaps leading to some form of depression and other emotional and health disaster. This is a dangerous imbalance.

We need clarity of vision of who we are in relation to our presence on this planet. We need to identify and understand our purpose and reason for being here. It is not enough to live from day-to-day without examining one's life's journey of choices and decisions. To not examine oneself is a dangerous imbalance.

For example, many people who go into business, work on developing a business plan, a blueprint to help them navigate the healthy growth of the business. Just as important for our life's journey, we need to also develop a plan for ourselves. We need to know where want to go and how to get there. Take a few moments and reflect on the fifteen questions I prepared for you in the next section of this book.

If you have not asked yourself these fifteen questions before, you need to ask them now. Address them and take note personal notes with which to reflect upon. It's your life, don't waste it.

It is never too late to begin living your life as it was supposed to lived. If you are interested in making money, look at your hobbies and see if you can begin to turn them into a positive, rewarding business venture. **We need to work to live, not live to work,** which is what many of us do. This is a dangerous imbalance.

We need to understand ourselves before trying to understand others. Begin to use the fifteen questions to improve the potential of your vision that will help you transform your life and establish an inner structure that depends on a system of **personal value-centered awareness.**

Once you get out the Box, and become liberated, you can begin to live your purpose, and part of that purpose, is for you to reach out and help others get out the Box. The magic to life is to give, not take. You must first be free to have that power.

You will be able to sing with the wind without being blown away, dance with the Sun without getting burned, and to have a positive impact on the lives of those you encounter. Balance always gives you pure and positive energy. Before I jumped out the Box, I used to focus on material things, making money and looking good on the outside while my balance of hearth and happiness was taking a beating. This was a dangerous imbalance.

I've utilized my life experiences to help establish an inner structure that depends on a system of personal value-centered awareness.

I had come to understand that when it rains, there is a purpose why it rains. Learn to turn your scars into stars.
When I experience joy, I know that it was my encounter with sadness that provided me an opportunity to better appreciate joy.

I know that when I laugh, there will also be moments when I must cry.

I know that when faced with the decision between a positive opportunity and a positive risk, I will take the risk. But know that **"risk"** is not impulse. It is the choice we make based on the truth we want to live.

I turned to my experiences, looking at my strength and weaknesses to help navigate my journey.

Balance is living your true purpose on the plant. I did my studies at the State University of New York at Buffalo (SUNYAB). As a student, I learned more outside the classroom then I did inside. I was a student leader, founder of the Puerto Rican student organization (PODER). As a student leader, **PODER** joined forces with the **Black Student Union** to confront the university administration to end racism on the campus, and to open the admission door to recruit Black and Puerto Rican students. We convince the university administration to establish an office of minority student affairs (OMSA). The office served as a link of contacts and resources for the local Black and Latino community.

The office was established, and I graduated with my BA degree that same year, and I accepted the position of associate director of the office. I used the position to educate myself, to learn about management, administration, and community relations. In that position, I established a relationship with the community's leading Black and Puerto Rican leaders, as well as with the local elected officials.

In addition, because I was the administration's liaison to the Black and Puerto Rican students and their organizations, I had an opportunity to work with them on the development of workshops, seminars, special community outreach, and in organizing conferences. One of my tasks was to assist in finding Black and Puerto Rican poets, writers, musicians, educators, and radicals (speakers/lecturers) to speak at the many of the programs or conferences sponsored by the students or administration.

In contacting the speakers' bureaus throughout the country, I found out that most speakers' bureaus had few, if any, Black or Latino speakers. From this experience, I found myself directing contacting Black and Latino poets, writers, elected officials, educators, business leaders, etc.

After twelve years at SUNYAB, I retired and completely divorced myself from higher education, but I always kept the idea of a speaker's bureau in the back of my mind. Twenty plus years later, I used that college experience to create the first Black & Latino Speakers Bureau in the country, known as AOC Speakers and Consultants, which I created in 1991. Later, it became Nubian Speakers.

After Nubian Speakers, there were several educationally related businesses that I worked on, based on my vision and concept. All the businesses that I organized, or invested were committed to educational, business and economic development – Don Pedro Cookies, Educational Pledge Partnership, The New Tomorrow (Loisiada), Festival del Libro (East Harlem), and La Fortaleza Project (East Harlem).

In 2013, I came back to Buffalo, NY, from the heart and soul of el Barrio, Spanish Harlem, presently known as East Harlem.

Since I came back, I've developed an advocate group (Puerto Rican Committee for Community Justice), a community publication (the Latino Village), and an art gallery (Campeche Art Gallery – Puerto Rican and Latino Fine Art).

My plan is simply to continue to enjoy living my life, but with a valued system of love and passion for giving and caring. I've always focused on the idea "to serve", and when the idea (gift) is executed with "care and love", harmony comes your way. It's like the idea or gift telling you, "I done it, I gave it, so I'm back."
If your goal is to only make money, then you may meet that goal, but ask yourself, "Will you have joy and harmony in your life if that is all you focus on?" You will miss the Balance.
If you can find it in you to learn to stay focused, balanced, and work to prepare a sound plan for your life journey, and you sincerely make sure to include your purpose to serve, destiny will come to support and move your efforts forward.

You will have the harmony, good health, and the music that only you can play because it was written and composed only by you, you found your purpose, you found your gift.

I dare and challenge you to work on your Balance. God's universe meant for you to enjoy the wonders of life with a base of spiritual balance. Go and enjoy the music, enjoy who you really are.

PASSING THE TORCH
Questions to Self-Discovery

The following sixteen (16) questions are designed to help with your self-development process. The questions also will work to develop clarity of vision who you are in relation to your presence on this planet. It is not enough to live day-to-day without examining one's life's journey of choice and decisions.

Take the time and provide answers to the following questions. If addressed seriously, these questions will help to enhance your purpose and quality of life.

Learn to truly appreciate why you are a living creature on this planet earth.

Get out of the Box --- and be you!

1. **WHO ARE YOU?** Use this question to challenge yourself to examine what you have become since the day of your birth. Begin to see how you can carve out the real you.

2. **WHY WERE YOU BORN?** Give thoughts to the reason you were born; Is it an accident or is there a spiritual or divine purpose for your existence. Are you here to give or to take? Take a good look at the events of the world and how you are linked and connected to them.

3. **ARE YOU LIVING YOUR DREAMS, DO YOU HAVE DREAMS?** Are you working as a doorman but want to be a painter? Are you living in a place and not happy about it? Are you employed in a job that you dislike but stay just to establish retirement benefits after 20 plus years on the job? Do not let your dreams to escape. Get on the road and move forward. Do not be afraid to take risks. Risks open doors, not taking risks keeps you where you are.

4. **WHAT ARE YOU DOING WITH YOUR LIFE AT THIS MOMENT?** Instead of saying "I hope my dreams come true", why not say, "I will work and plan to make my dreams come true." There is a reason for dreaming. Many of your dreams are like blueprints and designs. Do not let your dreams remain dreams. Bring them to life.

5. **ARE YOU LIVING A LIFE BASED ON OTHER PEOPLES' EXPECTATIONS?** Do what you need to be doing, and not what others want you to do. Remember that the expectations must come from you, and not from anyone else. You are the gatekeeper of your aspirations on this planet. The expectations are yours to design and navigate. Accept counseling and advice, but you must make the decisions and choices.

6. **ARE YOU HAPPY OR UNHAPPY?** Make up your mind to be happy. Do not allow or give your power away to others. Let no one direct or to control your emotions. Control your ego and understand the influence of family. Appreciate your association with the universe. Make up your mind to be happy.

7. **IS YOUR LIFE BASED ON AN OPPORTUNITY PROVIDED, OR ON A RISK YOU TOOK?** Are you cruising in life, taking anything that comes your way without an honest examination of yourself in relation to these opportunities? Work on things you would like to be doing, and what you need to do to get there. You need to enjoy the element of risk and let go of what you now have so you can move forward with your personal purpose and mission.

8. **HAVE YOU ENVISION YOUR LIFE 5, 10, OR 15 YEARS FROM NOW?** Stop cruising and begin to see yourself 5, 10, and 15 years from now. What do you see, or would like to see? This is the right moment to plant your seeds for your personal tree to grow, to enjoy the fruits of your labor 5, 10, and 15 years from now. The beauty or success of tomorrow never comes to those that don't take the time to design it.

9. **ARE YOU MAINTAINING A SYSTEM OF VALUES AND STANDARDS TO GOVERN YOUR LIFE?** How do you live your life from day-to-day? Is something inside you stopping you from doing what you need to be doing? How do you arrive at making important decisions, or choices? Are you taking the time to examine your life to secure your journey? What is a journey?

10. **ARE YOU A CONSUMER OR A PROVIDER, DO YOU KNOW THE DIFFERENCE?** A consumer consumes (takes). A provider provides

(gives). You need to address this question very seriously if you intend to move to a higher level of awareness and consciousness. The answer and your personal actions will be a big step in formulating the way you live your life.

11. **DO YOU UNDERSTAND YOUR STRENGTHS AND WEAKNESSES?** Examine yourself to understand your weaknesses and strengths of your human tools. As humans, we all have them. Work on introducing your weakness to your strength, and introduce your strength to your weakness, as they must work together. The sooner you learn and understand yourself, the more you grow and develop. Read, write, use the computer, attend lectures, get involved in your community, and ask questions. Just set things into motion.

12. **WHAT ARE YOUR HOBBIES?** Take the time to understand the origin of your interest in hobbies. Hobbies can be an extension of your mission, reason, and purpose for being on this planet. Properly utilized, hobbies can help you with your personal growth and development as a person.

13. **HAVE YOU EXPLORED THE POTENTIAL OF YOUR HOBBIES?** Hobbies are hidden treasures that can lead to a career or business venture. Get to understand the value of your hobbies and examine how they can help you grow and develop, spiritually and economically. You can become an entrepreneur, CEO, President; you can become a very important person of your community, or the country, just based on your hobby or hobbies.

14. **HAVE YOU GIVEN ANY THOUGHTS TO THE DIFFERENCE BETWEEN BEING RELIGIOUS AND BEING SPIRITUAL?** Many people believe in a God, and they attend a church for their religious guidance. Others do not attend a church, but also

believe, taking upon themselves the need to reach out and talk directly to God, connecting to the universe. What about you, are you a spiritual person, or are you a religious person, and can you be both? Always connect yourself to this question and maintain faith and respect to your origin. Always ask questions. Always strive to maintain a spiritual or religious foundation.

15. **DO YOU NEED TO MAKE FRIENDS WITH THE MIRROR?** Be happy with who you are. Understand your mind and body. Have the courage to say goodbye to your negative energy around you. If you are alive, you are in the game of life. Play by the rules or make the rules. Avoid living day-to-day without knowing where you're going.

16. **DO YOU KNOW THAT YOU HAVE A SPECIAL GIFT?** Remember that your reason and purpose for being here is a gift, but you must discover or find the gift. Use your vision, imagination, and creativity to find it, and once you find it, use it and give it away. Once you give it away, it always comes back for you to share again, and again and again.

The Educational Pledge of Allegiance

Making the Pledge

As you begin to reflect on the questions, take personal notes and begin to document your presence on the planet. It is never too late to begin living your life as it was supposed to be lived.

Every day is a gift to start again.

We need to understand ourselves before trying to understand others. Review the questions and utilize them to understand and improve the potential of your vision, a vision to help you transform your life and help you establish an inner structure that depends on a system of personal value-centered awareness.

It is never too late to make a U-turn, time to make the pledge...

The Educational Pledge
By Alberto O. Cappas

I pledge always to try my best to understand
The importance of knowledge and education

I pledge to paint a positive picture of where
I plan to be tomorrow
Not allowing obstacles to stop the growth of
My plans for the future

I pledge to maintain
A healthy mind and body
Staying away from the evil of drugs

I pledge to seek answers to questions
With the understanding that they
Will lead to other discoveries

I pledge to work diligently
With the awareness and confidence
That hard work today will serve
As the seeds for my strong tree tomorrow
A tree that no one will be able to tear down

I pledge to learn proper languages
Beginning with the language of my Mother
Always prepared to appreciate others

I pledge to gain a better understanding of
who I am
By understanding my Cultural roots
To fully accept who I am
As a spiritual and human being
A rainbow of many cultures and colors

I pledge to overcome any personal misfortunes
Becoming stronger from such misfortunes

Always striving to become
A compassionate and wise person

I pledge, I pledge, I pledge.

About the Author

Alberto O. Cappas

Alberto O. Cappas, graduate of the State University of NY@ Buffalo (1968-1972). Worked as Associate Director of UB's Office of Minority Student Affairs (1971-1978), Founder of UB's Puerto Rican Student organization (PODER), several Puerto Rican Community Organizations in Buffalo's local communities (Virginia Street Puerto Rican Parade & Carnival, Puerto Rican-Chicano Committee of Build, Inc., WBFO-FM Spanish Programing, The Latin Journal, and served as the 'go to person' in several political campaigns.

After many years of Buffalo community involvement (1970-1983), he returned to New York City to continue his progressive style of community involvement. In 1984, Gov. Mario Cuomo appointed Cappas as Deputy Commissioner of Communications & Special Projects for the New York State Division for Youth.

His most recent literary work is included in **"The City That Never Sleeps, Poems of New York"** -- published by the University Press (SUNYAB)

In NYC, he dedicated some of his time to writing, publishing "Dona Julia: A collection of his published poems."

He served on several New York City Puerto Rican community boards in Loisiada and in East Harlem.

He published two newspaper, one in the lower east side (The New Tomorrow), and the other in East Harlem (East Harlem Journal). He is also the creator of "El Festival del Libro" (East Harlem First Annual Festival of Books), and "La Fortaleza", a business and economic development concept with an arts and cultural theme. He was also the founder of AOC Speakers Bureau, securing speaking engagements for Black and Puerto Rican Poets, Writers, Artists, and other fields.

Cappas retired from public service in 2010 after working with NYC Health & Hospital Corporation, and the NYC Human Resource Administration (HRA).

He now lives in Buffalo, NY with his wife, Ramona. Alberto is a creative and imaginative spirit, responsible for tons of organizations and programs in operation today.

This book (2nd edition), and the **Educational Pledge,** is his most important work, as he says, "it has touched the minds of so many young people, many of them now doctors, engineers, teachers, community leaders, poets, and writers.

Alberto is the author of *"To Think is to Grow, Quotes to Provoke the Mind",* self-published this past year (2017). The book is based on his original quotes he has written throughout the years. He is also the author of a small handbook, *"Entering the Universe: The Educational Pledge, Basic Questions to Jumpstart the Mind, a 20-page manual for school orientations and workshops.*

He is the founder of the **Puerto Rican Committee for Community Justice** (PRCCJ), and co-publisher of the **Latino Village,** a Buffalo monthly publication, published in partnership with his wife, Ramona Cappas. He is also an original founding member of *Campeche Art Travelling Gallery*, a new art and cultural institution — a Puerto Rican & Latino Fine Art Gallery, located in Buffalo, NY.

At seventy-three years, Alberto would like to pass the touch to someone to continue the vision, message, and the roots of this book – the reason for the 2nd edition, which also includes the well-known poem, the Educational Pledge.

"This educational pledge has done wonders for many, and I would like to see it in our public schools and colleges, where it's greatly needed. I hope to see **the Educational Pledge** reach the minds of our children and youth before I move on to my next journey."

Final Thoughts:
MANIFEST DIVERSITY

By Solomon Joseph

Diversify, Diverse, & Diversified:
Heart and Soul of Diversity

Manifest Diversity

While I believe and hope to see the Educational Pledge reach the classrooms of our students, I also want to see **"Manifest Diversity"** reach the heart and soul of all the difference American Cultures.

We have many differences, but we all smile, laugh and cry in the same language.

It is far better to accept and understand each other's differences instead of closing ourselves to people who look, talk and act different from us.

We can all learn from one another. These beautiful messages shared by each culture and ethnic group is a message for us all. Its main theme is love. Love for all humanity. Love for every human being.

Love has no dominant race, color or creed. Love is universal. Love unites us, brings us closer, and creates an understanding fueled with compassion, respect and appreciation. So, when we don't have love for each other it leads to hate and hate divides. Within hate we have, racism, prejudice, disrespect and other negative feelings which divide us.

With everything that's happened, and is still happening, it doesn't benefit us to hate. It doesn't benefit us at all. Hate doesn't progress humanity. Hate takes us so many steps far back that we must start all over again. We are not living in the past anymore.

This country has been built on the backs of men, women and children of all ages and races. We are now living amongst each other, loving each other, laughing with each other, crying with each other, eating with each other and sharing resources with each other… why? Because we learned to co-exist.

We learned to understand the value of being human. We learned to appreciate one another because we know that there was a time when there was no humanity, no equality, no compassion and no appreciation. So, let us take a moment now to give thanks and honor the men, women and children who fought hard for justice, equality, peace and diversity to be achieved. Let us pay homage to our brothers and sisters who pioneered the way for our world to be an inclusive environment.

We don't have to fight each other. We don't always have to turn every disagreement into an argument. Putting others down because we need to feel better about ourselves doesn't create a harmonious environment. It creates a negative environment and that's where hate comes in and the worst you can do is turn an argument into hate.

There is such a thing as agreeing to disagree. And that's ok. It's ok to disagree. We are human, we can form our own opinions, think our own thoughts, feel our own feelings but it doesn't make us wrong. It just makes us different. Being different doesn't make you wrong.

That's why Manifest Diversity is important, because it's being shown that we can all live together, even with our differences. With so many cultures, races and ethnic groups from around the world isn't it exciting we all share this beautiful earth with each other?

Isn't it exciting that we can talk to different people, listen and dance to different music and taste different foods? It's pretty darn amazing and It's beautiful because we are living a multicultural society. A very colorful society.

Please, open your heart and mind, open your eyes and you will see, you will feel and believe the true colors of every living thing in this world. Ladies and gentlemen, we are meant to live in unity, not division, because there is more strength in unity, and there is more strength in diversity. Together we can manifest diversity.

In closing, I would like to thank Mr. Alberto O. Cappas, author of the **Educational Pledge**, for passing me the torch, starting by letting me write an introduction to his book, and for giving me an opportunity to introduce my **"Manifest Diversity."**

About Solomon Joseph

Solomon Joseph is an educator, founder of the **Manifest Diversity** project, whose mission is to teach and share positive

and meaningful information and lessons about the significance of understanding "Diversity" and how to apply it in our daily lives. Solomon loves to interact with young people.

Solomon was born and raised in Washington Heights, adopting Puerto Ricans/Dominicans as his family. Solomon's parents are from Pakistan. While Solomon maintains his cultural roots, he has learned, adopted and embraced cultures from around the world, providing him the ingredients to understand the essence of "Manifest Diversity."

He will be carrying the torch of "The Educational Pledge" to inspire and light up the lives of the present and future generations.

To contact him for workshops, seminars and speaking engagements for your class or school, contact him at theeducationalpledge@gmail.com. Visit his site at theeducationalpledge.com

The impact of the Educational Pledge

-Reviews-

THE POWER OF THE EDUCATIONAL PLEDGE

"The pledge will deliver a special message to our youth, parents, teachers, educator, community leaders, civic and public officials. I wish I had this poem with me when I was young."

J. Enrique Rodriguez, Bronx, NY

'Regarding youth training, I look forward to sharing the Educational Pledge   with others. I'm currently training a group of teachers in LSCL, so I will pass the information along."

Mike Perry Garden Grove, CA

"I just wanted to compliment you on the wonderful and inspirational message (The Pledge). We need to keep re-enforcing positive thoughts to our young people, and this pledge hits the spot."

Irma Thompson, NYC, NY

"As a parent, The Pledge is excellent, so real! I gave to my daughter and she framed it."

Ilene Acevedo, Queens, NY

"I just wanted to say thanks for the beautiful work you do, particularly around children's education. I've shared the pledge with many people, especially online."

Raquel Rivera, Lower East Side, NY

"I have followed your career pursuits with interest in my own way only because you have demonstrated a never give up spirit. This is the attitude we must convey to our youth. I must save your pledge, and I will share with others on how to bring

to life the words in your work."
Eric Toro, Bronx, NY

"I am emailing you because I am interested in including The Pledge in our PHIOTA Newspaper. Over 4,000 copies will be published, and we believe, that it will assist in giving exposure in the Latino community, as well as Colleges and Universities."

Elizer Hernandez,
National President, Phi Iota Alpha Fraternity, Inc.

"Your pledge is very inspiring to me as a youth development professional. I hope that it is reaching many youths and that they too are inspired by your work."

Frank Sanchez, Texas

"The Pledge is very powerful, very inspiring, and very through-provoking."

Indhira Marichal, Albany, NY

"The Pledge provided me with the encouragement I much needed to continue with working with children. I am a Kindergarten public school teacher in the South Bronx."

Carlos M. Lopez, Bronx, NY

"The pledge is a reflective tool to help anyone, both young and old. Give someone the gift of self-empowerment and elf-realization by sharing the questions and the ultimate answers that come with such quest. It is a life time gift. It truly transcends generations. I encourage parents, educators, young people and everyone to share the book (Never too late to make a U-turn) with their friends and love ones. It is a conduit for personal growth."

Angelica Aquino, Attorney, Washington Heights, NY.

"The Pledge is a must-read lesson for all. I truly recommend it. Mr. Cappas' insightful and clear message is one that will motivate everyone to start "thinking creatively.""

Rafael Rodriguez, Queens, NY

"I send you a million thank you for providing me with your work. It brings many aspects of real life to my awareness. I have showed your work to my professor, and they too, have enjoyed it."

Gabriel Vazquez, Brooklyn, NY

"I have just finished reading the Educational Pledge that was sent to me through the Phi Iota Alpha Fraternity email system. We can never forget who we are, and we must never allow the youth to do that either."

Michelle L. Moore-Diaz, Buffalo, NY

"I loved the pledge and think it creates a positive vision for our children, especially since it addresses the 'understanding my cultural roots', which I believe can give strength to many. Is this pledge in Spanish? I have many Spanish-speaking parents and students who can benefit from this message."

Carmen S. Vasquez, Hosto Community College (CUNY)

"I pledge your pledge from my very soul. That is such an awesome poem! I love it."

Chirindy, Phaedra

"It is an honor for me to include our Pledge in our publication. I am grateful that you took the time to write this Pledge. I strongly believe that our young people need words of encouragement, support and positive role models."

**Deyanira Barrios, President,
National Latina Women's League, Washington, DC**

"Our schools are staffed with over 800 full-time Substance Abuse Prevention Intervention Specialists who provide services to all our students. I have asked the citywide director of these programs to share The Pledge with the directors of the community school district programs at their next meeting. I am sure that they will find it to be a valuable tool for use with our students."

Francine B. Goldstein, NYC Board of Education, NYC, NY

"The Educational Pledge is highly recommended for adoption in our inner-city public schools in the interest of our children. The Pledge teaches the essential roles that values, and standards play in the planning of one's successful journey in life."

Editor, Latina Voices publication

"I found The Pledge to be inspirational for all children, not just those of Hispanic descent. Success is bound to follow increased knowledge, hard work, and understanding of self and appreciation of others."

Lauren Bradway, Neptune Beach, Fl.

"The Pledge is a very deep poem and I am a true believer with what it says. I changed my life, once I met my father for the first time. My faith, my religion, and my whole way of life changed for the better. This Pledge is the true essence of what I am all about."

Carlos Javier Jimenez Nieves, Brooklyn, NY

The Pledge in Action

Sharing

Educational Pledge at Community Day, sponsored by Northwest Bank Connecticut Street Branch

Pull-up your Pants Poster

Pull-Up your Pants Institute

An Institute for Personal
Development

Please help in development of this idea.
Please Share & Post!

What you get when you enlist:

⇨ **Come and enjoy the benefits of growing up**

⇨ **Come and learn about the history of where this style came from**

⇨ **Free Belts to hold up your pants and Manhood**

⇨ **Come and learn about your rich Culture & Tradition**

⇨ **Get assistance in obtaining employment or business ownership opportunities**

⇨ **Get assistance in getting an Education**

⇨ **An opportunity to start a new life**

⇨ **An opportunity to meet new friends**

⇨ **An opportunity to get your personal life together**

⇨ **An opportunity to learn to Dress**

⇨ **An opportunity to learn about yourself**

Call US Today:
Alberto O. Cappas, **Co-Chair**
Jose C. Pizarro, **Co-Chair**
Committee to Change our Future by reaching out to our young people

ATTENTION COMMUNITY ORGANIZATIONS AND COMMUNITY LEADERS:

WE NEED VOLUNTEERS
IDEA IN DEVELOPMENT

Educational Pledge Certificate of Achievement

Certificate of Achievement
Presented to

_____

In Recognition of your Decision to
Take The Pledge and Witness
A Positive Advancement in your Lifetime
Month Year

Take the Pledge Recognition Committee
The Educational Pledge Partnership

_____

Solomon Joseph
President

Meet, Define, and Discuss Board

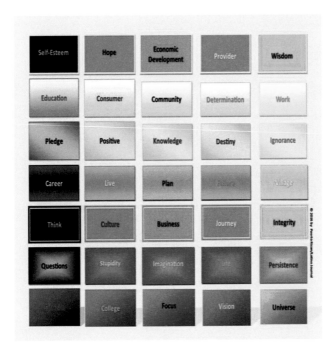

BUFFALO LATINO VILLAGE
CONFIRMS NEW EDITOR

Solomon Joseph, founder of Manifest Diversity, accepted the position as editor of the Buffalo Latino Village, starring with the March 2019 issue. Officially, he joined the Village staff this past month as a columnist, dedicated to educational and diversity related themes. Solomon, originally from India, was raised in New York City's Washington Heights, where he learned about Puerto Rican and Dominican culture.

Manifest Diversity provides seminars and workshops aimed at bringing people of all cultures together. He recently assumed responsibilities for the **Educational Pledge**, another project that works directly with parents and youth in dealing with self-development, self-pride, and positive values, also aimed at re-directing the lives of young people "at risk" of entering a negative path in their lives.

Ramona Karydis-Cappas, co-publisher, said that "the Buffalo Latino Village is very fortunate to have Solomon as editor of the publication. He brings new energy and new ideas as a member of the young generation. We are definitely passing the torch to the young generation."

Solomon Joseph Preparing for an Educational Pledge Presentation

All Together makes a happy Planet
"Manifest Diversity"
Diversify and Diversified

I Pledge!

Miguel A. Montes
Educational Pledge in Action….

The Educational Pledge Prescription

A Letter from a Parent

An email to the Educational Pledge

Monday, May 9, 2011

Mr. Cappas,

I just wanted to take this opportunity to say that my daughter is soooo excited about receiving her certificate in the mail. She said the following:

"Mami, something special happened. I got a certificate in the mail with my name on it. Here, I'll read it to you."

She reads it to me then says, *"I put it on the fridge and read it every day over and over. It helps me want to keep doing good so I can go to college and have a career."*

I can't even begin to tell you how good that makes me feel as a parent. I get emotional just thinking about it. Thanks for doing that for her. It means a lot to me. She said she's going to read the books you sent her as well. You're doing a great thing with our youth and I applaud your hard work and dedication. It's amazing what we can accomplish... one youth at a time. Thanks again Mr. Cappas!!! You're a blessing!!!

~Tanya

The Educational Pledge Poster

"I pledge to fully accept who I'm as a spiritual and human being, a rainbow of many cultures and colors...."

The Educational Pledge

Poster Available in 12 x 18, hard & glossy paper—only $10.00
Payable to The Educational Pledge, PO Box 742, Buffalo, NY 14209
Information: Solomon Joseph, theeducationalpledge@gmail.com

Puerto Rican Parade in New York City

Cappas & Montes
"The Beginning"

Cappas reciting the Pledge...

Miguel A. Montes
Passing the torch to the next Educational Pledge generation

Alberto O. Cappas
"Passing the Torch"

Alberto O. Cappas

Solomon Joseph
"Accepting the Torch"

Solomon Joseph

Sharing the Torch"

The Educational Pledge
Banner

Making the "Pledge"
-Pine Harbor Workshop-

Sister and Brother
Make the "Pledge"
-Pine Harbor Workshop-

Educational Pledge Certificate
-Pine Harbor Workshop-

Showing the Educational Pledge Magnet
-Pine Harbor Workshop-

The Educational Pledge Workshop

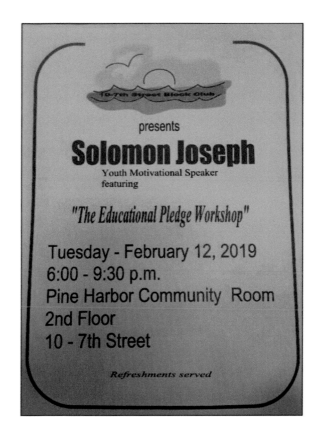

Educational Pledge at the Leadership Academy

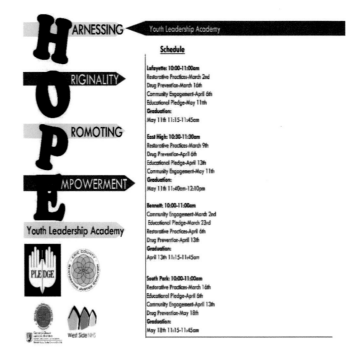

HARNESSING

Youth Leadership Academy

ORIGINALITY

PROMOTING

EMPOWERMENT

Youth Leadership Academy

PLEDGE

West Side NHS

Schedule

Lafayette: 10:00-11:00am
Restorative Practices-March 2nd
Drug Prevention-March 16th
Community Engagement-April 6th
Educational Pledge-May 11th
Graduation:
May 11th 11:15-11:45am

East High: 10:30-11:30am
Restorative Practices-March 9th
Drug Prevention-April 6th
Educational Pledge-April 13th
Community Engagement-May 11th
Graduation:
May 11th 11:40am-12:10pm

Bennett: 10:00-11:00am
Community Engagement-March 2nd
Educational Pledge-March 23rd
Restorative Practices-April 13th
Drug Prevention-April 13th
Graduation:
April 13th 11:15-11:45am

South Park: 10:00-11:00am
Restorative Practices-March 16th
Educational Pledge-April 6th
Community Engagement-April 13th
Drug Prevention-May 18th
Graduation:
May 18th 11:15-11:45am

Using your Name to Guide you
In the journey

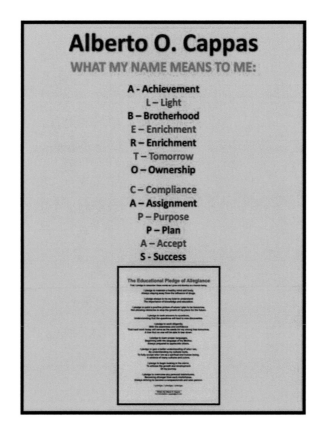

Reciting the Pledge
-Pine Harbor Workshop-

THE EDUCATIONAL PLEDGE FEVER AT THE PINE HARBOR APARTMENTS
CONTACT US TO VISIT YOUR SCHOOL; EXPERIENCE THE ENERGY OF THE EDUCATIONAL PLEDGE
SOLOMON JOSEPH, SPEAKER/PRESENTER
EMAIL: THEEDUCATIONALPLEDGE@GMAIL.COM / WEBSITE: THEEDUCATIONALPLEDGE.COM

Educational Pledge Tools

Educational Pledge Tools

The Educational Pledge
Cap

Receiving the Educational Pledge Certificate, with copy of book: "Never too late to make a U-turn", by Alberto O. Cappas

Spanish Version

Por Alberto O. Cappas

La Promesa Educacional

DEDICADO A LOS NINOS Y FAMILIAS

Yo prometo mantener
Mente y cuerpo saludable
Alejandome del maligno vicio de las drogas
Prometo siempre esforzarme para mejor comprender
La importancia del conocimiento y la educación
Pintando un retrato positivo hacia donde
Pienso estar mañana
No permitiendo obstaculos que tronchen el desarrollo
De mis proyectos hacia el futuro
Prometo buscar respuestas a mis preguntas
Comprendiendo que las repuestas a preguntas
A veces nos llevan a otros descubrimientos
Prometo trabajar con esfuerzo
Con el conocimiento y confianza
Que el trabajo arduo hoy servirá
Como semillas para el árbol fuerte del mañana
Un árbol que jamás se podrá arrancar
Prometo aprender idiomas correctamente
Comenzando con el de mi madre
Siempre dispuesto a apreciar los de otros
Prometo lograr mejor conocimiento de mi persona
Con el conocimiento de mis raices culturales
Aceptando quién soy como ser espiritual y ser humano
Un arco iris de varias culturas y colores
Prometo vencer mis desgracias personales
Haciéndome más fuerte por las desdichas
Siempre esforzándome hacia la potencialidad
De ser una persona de
compacion y sabia.

Translated by Coral Caporale, JD

The Educational Pledge available for Speaking and Workshop Engagements

Theeducationalpledge.com

Educational Pledge Notepad:
Taking Notes to guide your
Educational Journey

Educational Pledge Notepad

Compliments of theeducationalpledge.com

NOTEPAD

NOTEPAD

NOTEPAD

NOTEPAD

NOTEPAD

_____

_____

_____

_____

_____

_____

_____

_____

_____

_____

_____

_____

_____

_____

_____

_____

_____

_____

_____

NOTEPAD

NOTEPAD

NOTEPAD

"Diversify, Diverse, and Diversified Heart and Soul of Diversity"

Solomon Joseph

THE EDUCATIONAL PLEDGE:
Questions to Self-Development

Copyright © 2019 by Alberto O. Cappas

ISBN: 9781793894908

Buffalo Latino Village Press
PO Box 742
Buffalo, NY 14209

Buffalolatinovillage.com

A Publication of the Manifest Diversity Series

Credit:

Photos from the Educational Pledge Workshops at
the Pine Harbor Apartments,
Buffalo, NY, were made possible by the
Pine Harbor Tenants Club, coordinated by
Dinah Aponte, President.